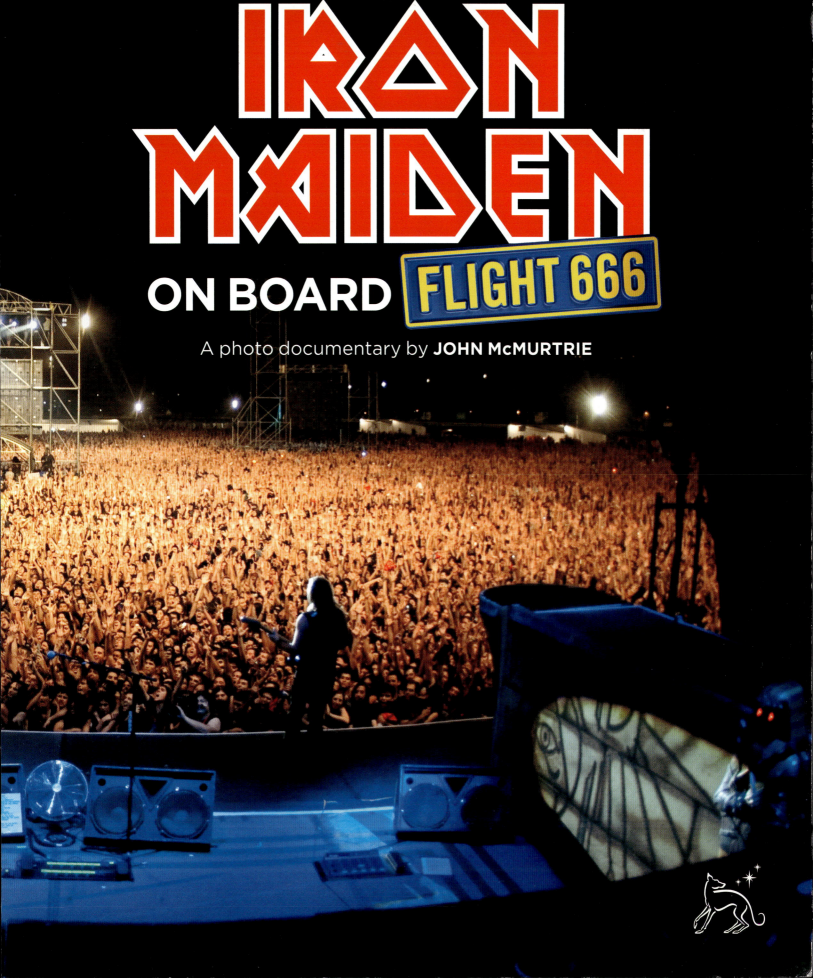

CONTENTS

Foreword by **BRUCE DICKINSON** 6
Introduction by **JOHN McMURTRIE** 9

Highlights from

SOMEWHERE BACK IN TIME
WORLD TOUR 2008-09

AND

THE FINAL FRONTIER
WORLD TOUR 2010-11

FOREWORD BY **BRUCE DICKINSON**

The idea of ED FORCE ONE, a flying tour bus with band, crew and equipment on the same aircraft, came to me when I was a solo artist. We flew around America in a very old, low and slow piston engined Piper Navajo, six of us and a drum kit precariously lashed to the insides. Fast forward 10 years. After two years flying the band on the "Bruce Goose" a Cessna 421 seven seater, I ended up flying 757s and 737s for Astraeus Airlines and had moved to the Captain's seat. I asked our then Director of Flight Operations, John Mahon, what it would take to secure equipment down the back of a 757 instead of passenger seats. Being Irish, John reflected back to his days as a loader on DC-3 Dakotas flying nightfreight newspapers in and out of Dublin. "Ahh just a big 9G Cargo Net...that should do it...." It turned out to be a bit more complicated than that.

〉〉〉〉〉〉

I had just mooted the idea to IRON MAIDEN Manager Rod Smallwood – the advantages were several. Essentially the globe would be reduced to the equivalent of a North American tour. The delays and costs associated with freight, customs and inconvenient airline schedules would be circumvented and territories which hitherto had been deemed "uneconomical" for the band to tour, could now be included. Mr Mercator and every schoolboy's map of the world went out the window and we bought ourselves a large globe. The next question was, which way round to go? Conventional wisdom said that it is better to go west around the world as this way you gain time. Being essentially unconventional, I disagreed. The prevailing winds would save 10% of time and

fuel if we went eastbound – a considerable sum – but even more compelling was time and jet lag. On a 6 or 8 week tour, jet lag would be more or less continuous. The crucial factor was to adjust our bodies so that we were alert at 9pm local time every day – stage time. The range and distances we would cover meant that the maximum time change over any 2 days would be 5 hours – ie we would arrive at 10pm our time, and in fact it would be 3am local. So...after a couple of beers we go to bed at 1am (our time) as the sun rises locally!! Waking up after a solid 8 hours rest at 10 o'clock (our time) but... oh dear 3pm local...what on earth is going on? By 9pm locally our bodies are thinking "OK 4pm in the afternoon. I could cope with running round and doing a gig..." Conversely, trying to do the same thing eastbound (New York for example) we would be wide awake at 6am and at 9pm our bodies would be telling us to go to sleep. The next hurdle was to persuade agents and promoters to think outside of their comfort zone..."Mumbai to Perth? You can't do that! You'd need a time machine..." and of course that's exactly what ED FORCE ONE is – a time machine.

〉〉〉〉〉〉

The 757 is one of Mr Boeing's most elegant creations. It has the lines of a bird of prey, an extraordinary conjoining of engineering and aesthetics. Talk to most pilots and ask if they would like to fly a 757 and most likely a gleam would appear in their eye. The 757 though is no spring chicken. The last one came off the production line in 2005, and many question why Boeing don't still make them. Simply, there is no replacement for a 757 in the world except another

757. It is more than half British; it's wing was a British design that flew on the Hawker Siddeley Trident and its two Rolls-Royce RB211E4 engines provide a massive thrust to weight ratio. At full thrust on a lightly laden aircraft, ED FORCE ONE is climbing at over 7000 feet per minute, more than 60 miles an hour vertically – there are jet fighters that can't do that. It will then cruise at 80% of the speed of sound for almost 8 hours and still land with international standard fuel reserves. When you are on holiday in your airbus or 737 and land, bear in mind that a 757 can land in half that distance, and when your 737 or airbus is stuck on the ground because of weather, a 757 can often go almost unrestricted. The 757 is a beast. And the number of this beast is ED FORCE ONE.

〉〉〉〉〉〉

Earlier there was talk of newspapers and netting for securing our freight on ED FORCE ONE. If only it were possible. ED FORCE ONE was a groundbreaking enterprise. Technically, operationally and politically. Let's start with the politics. ED FORCE ONE coincided with a new regime governing all aviation in Europe – E.A.S.A. We would be the first modification to an aircraft to be fully approved by the new regulator, so we had to expect rigorous auditing and forensic attention to detail. Technically our "cargo net" had morphed into an entirely different set of rules. New rules dictated that all cargo had to be secured in a totally fireproof compartment. The whole idea that made ED FORCE ONE viable was that we could change it from 221 passengers to our combi-format and back again – how could we achieve a "fireproof containment vessel" and

still not destroy the passenger cabin? Lastly there were many operational changes to plan and train for. We would be flying across The Andes, landing in Quito at very high elevations, as well as Bogota which all required special simulator training. The loading and unloading of ED FORCE ONE would be very specific and require special procedures, especially with regard to distribution of fuel. Finally the Cabin Crew would all have to be trained in the new format and in the new locations of emergency equipment. Whilst all Astraeus Cabin Crew provide a terrific service, people often have no idea how rigorously they are trained to provide their primary function – which is safety.

〉〉〉〉〉〉

To facilitate all of this required more than 6 months of intense planning and some very fraught moments. Gradually the obstacles were overcome and it was a painstaking process inching towards our certification goal rather than leaping out of our baths like Archimedes and crying "Eureka!" There were comedic moments. The test day for the fireproof bags came. These bags sit atop the steel plates in the former passenger cabin at the rear of ED FORCE ONE. The idea was that in the event of the cargo catching fire, it would be unable to breach the material and as an aside, any smoke would be cleared and not contaminate the passenger cabin. So far so good, and the day of testing arrived. Solemn "Men From The Ministry" stood around a forlorn-looking fireproof bag on a freezing winter's day as engineers and firemen attempted to sustain a fire in it. Alas, the bag was so effective that any fire was almost immediately extinguished. This was unsatisfactory, so the bag

was subjected finally to a hail of Molotov cocktails in an effort to damage it. After 2 hours the men in suits departed, apparently satisfied. The outside of the bag moreover, never even became warm. They returned later, to embark on the enjoyable pursuit of lobbing smoke bombs into the back of the airliner in the hope of asphyxiating its occupants in the forward cabins. Mr Boeing's Smoke Clearance System worked as advertised, and the project was a go! As the reality sank in that we were going to do this after all, the media buzz started. The ED FORCE ONE name itself came from particularly inspired fans responding to a naming competition on the Maiden website and seized the imagination. The Powerslave-inspired livery of the 'Somewhere Back In Time World Tour' looked sensational on paper and was simply awesome in the flesh. Indeed, I was worried that The Final Frontier livery would not live up to its predecessor. Silly me. The media event that was ED FORCE ONE followed us round the world. Never mind being a rock 'n' roll band, our arrival was almost Presidential in many countries, making primetime news locally as well as CNN, Sky, Fox and ABC news globally.

>>>>>>

So what is it like to Captain ED FORCE ONE? Well, first of all I'm one of 3 pilots on board as well as 2 engineers and 4 cabin crew, plus a ground handling coordinator and a loadmaster. I fly typically around 30% of the flights. The rest of the time I am available as a back-up in the event of sickness or incapacitation (as happened on the way from Mumbai to Perth when food poisoning struck a crew member). Sadly this meant I was never able to sample Nicko's vintage wine selection in flight. On the other hand, I always arrived at the destination without a hangover! As Captain I'm responsible for everything that goes on aboard the aircraft, even if the mistake is someone else's! I have a great team to work with and to get the best out of people I believe in speaking openly about concerns and keeping information free-flowing between us all. The Captain's job is as much about management as it is about flying. Now that may not sound romantic, but it's actually very rewarding to identify and solve problems…before they become problems. It's an old adage but the saying 'A Captain using his knowledge and experience to ensure he never has to use his knowledge and experience' is especially applicable to unusual situations like ED FORCE ONE. As for the experience of flying, well this is too short an article to go on about it in length, except to say that I wrote a song about it. I played it to lots of my Airline chums and got a pretty decent thumbs-up. So the lyrics to 'Coming Home' are as close as I can get to the experience other than inviting you up there alongside me to share the experience. On a last point of interest, if you are curious as to what countries you can cover with the span of your hand at 41,000 feet – Belgium sprang to mind. One dark night with Brussels spread below like fluorescent yellow brain coral…. If that conjures up an image, terrific. If not, that's what this book is for. John McMurtrie captured in pictures all things I've probably forgotten and then some. Here it all is; in fact, if it's not in here, it probably never happened! Have fun out there… tailwinds and happy landings to you all!

Bruce Dickinson

INTRODUCTION BY **JOHN MCMURTRIE**

I will never forget the feeling at London Stansted Airport in 2008 as ED FORCE ONE throttled back and we thundered down the runway for the very first time. Everyone had the same look on their face. A combination of excitement, trepidation and down right terror. As the airport whizzed past my window I remember worrying if I had packed all my photographic gear. Lenses, camera bodies, batteries, laptop, hard drives. There was no way I had left anything behind, because we had been preparing for this for the last few months. I then tried to rationalise what we were about to do.

We are going on an adventure and the lead singer of IRON MAIDEN is at the controls!

Apparently Bruce knows what he is doing up front, he's passed all the relevant exams and they made him a captain. Are they mad? We are talking about the 'Bruce Bullet', the one who screams across the stage, tells crazy stories in the bar and drives cars way too fast! As we reach the end of the runway and ED FORCE ONE lifts into the air it dawns on me how historic this all is. Travelling twice around the world on board a customised Boeing 757 piloted by the lead singer of a heavy metal band. IRON MAIDEN have never done things by halves and have constantly taken things to a higher level. This big adventure is no exception and it's 30,000 feet higher! I am no stranger to touring, having worked as a music photographer for the last 2 decades. I have been on the road with bands many times before, on buses and the odd

private jet, but to embark on a journey this ambitious is something else; it is staggering.

It turns out Bruce knows exactly what he is doing. He has been flying now for 20 years, 10 of those on commercial jets and has accumulated over 7000 flying hours. We are in safe hands.

This book isn't just a snapshot of a band at their peak but a journal of 6 individuals who simply want to play to their fans in every corner of the globe and how they achieved it. My part as the photographer is to capture that journey as it unfolds. One hundred percent of the photographs in this book are moments as they happened. Not 'set-ups' or 'photo calls', just IRON MAIDEN being honest and doing what they do. Sometimes, even I struggled to keep up with the band's movements on a day to day basis. One minute we are flying, and then the next, Janick is out sight seeing, Steve is playing football, Adrian tennis, Dave and Nicko golfing and Bruce could be out doing one of a thousand activities! But what is guaranteed every night when IRON MAIDEN step out on stage, is a spectacular show with energy and passion. As a photographer you couldn't ask for a better subject to shoot.

I liken touring with IRON MAIDEN to that of a white knuckle ride at a theme park. You spend most of the time screaming and holding on for dear life. But when it comes to an end you just want to do it again, again, again!

John McMurtrie

IRON MAIDEN MASCOT 'EDDIE'

BRUCE DICKINSON

NICKO McBRAIN

STEVE HARRIS

ADRIAN SMITH

JANICK GERS

DAVE MURRAY

The newly decorated tail fin of ED FORCE ONE pokes out of a busy hangar on an airfield in Hampshire. Inside, the Boeing 757 is being inspected by Bruce as the modifications are completed. Trucks arrive for a dry run of loading and unloading the plane.

Will the elaborate stage set, all of IRON MAIDEN's instruments plus the complex sound equipment, fit in the customised plane?

Flight cases are stacked up on pallets and a single fork-lift truck begins the slow process of loading the cargo bays. After several hours of careful manoeuvring, 12 tonnes of equipment has been loaded. It fits! It will be another month before ED FORCE ONE is finally ready for its maiden voyage.

On a cold Christmas Eve in 2007 ED FORCE ONE leaves the hangar and takes off for Gatwick Airport, England. The aircraft now has to be approved for transit by the European aviation authorities.

SOMEWHERE BACK IN TIME
WORLD TOUR 2008

FEATURING HIGHLIGHTS FROM THE FIRST LEG ON BOARD ED FORCE ONE

FEBRUARY 2008
1ST MUMBAI, INDIA
4TH PERTH, AUSTRALIA
6TH MELBOURNE, AUSTRALIA
7TH MELBOURNE, AUSTRALIA
9TH SYDNEY, AUSTRALIA
10TH SYDNEY, AUSTRALIA
12TH BRISBANE, AUSTRALIA
15TH YOKOHAMA, JAPAN
16TH TOKYO, JAPAN
19TH LOS ANGELES, CA, USA
21ST GUADALAJARA, MEXICO
22ND MONTERREY, MEXICO

24TH MEXICO CITY, MEXICO
26TH SAN JOSE, COSTA RICA
28TH BOGOTA, COLOMBIA

MARCH 2008
2ND SAO PAULO, BRAZIL
4TH CURITIBA, BRAZIL
5TH PORTO ALEGRE, BRAZIL
7TH BUENOS AIRES, ARGENTINA
9TH SANTIAGO, CHILE
12TH SAN JUAN, PUERTO RICO
14TH NEW JERSEY, NJ, USA
16TH TORONTO, CANADA

7:30am: Dawn breaks at Stansted airport as the final pre-flight checks take place. Only hours earlier at 2am the Aviation Authority finally gave ED FORCE ONE permission to travel fully loaded with cargo and passengers. The aircraft has passed the stringent safety checks but only just in the nick of time. The remaining cargo can now be loaded, the band and crew begin boarding. ABOVE: Bruce and co-pilot John Haile check the flight plans as the remaining members of IRON MAIDEN arrive and see the customised aircraft for the very first time. RIGHT & BELOW: Adrian Smith, Dave Murray and Manager Rod Smallwood step aboard. Nicko receives a last minute delivery of fine wines, much to his approval.

ABOVE: Captain Bruce Dickinson welcomes everyone on board Flight 666 and promises that it will be a very exciting journey.

LEFT: All baggage loaded and Bruce gets the thumbs up from ground crew that ED FORCE ONE is ready to depart. Months of planning have led to this moment in time and Flight 666 departs London, Stansted airport at 09:58am, destination Mumbai, India.

Flying via Baku to refuel, ED FORCE ONE touches down in Mumbai at 2am. Although it is early there are many fans within the airport to welcome the band and even more outside. RIGHT: The following day Steve, Dave and Janick sample the sights, sounds and smells of Bombay, stopping at several temples and at the Gateway to India. After a few hours of sightseeing, the band party are whisked back to the hotel for a press conference with India's enthusiastic media.

1ST FEBRUARY 2008. Finally, after months of preparation, it is show day. RIGHT: The band arrive for a rare sound check and a production rehearsal.

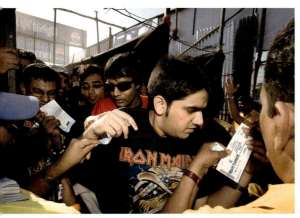

TOP LEFT: Although the stage is made from unconventional materials (bamboo and wooden planks) everyone is very satisfied with arrangements.

OPPOSITE LEFT: The word is given to open the doors to the mass of fans outside.

BELOW: IRON MAIDEN take to the stage at 8.30pm for the very first show of the Somewhere Back in Time World Tour.

1ST FEBRUARY 2008. Bandra Kurla Complex, Mumbai, India.

7am: After 12 hours of travelling, IRON MAIDEN arrive in Australia to a heartfelt welcome on their first visit since 1992. A longer than anticipated refuel in Jakarta has resulted in touch down being 5 hours later than expected. BELOW: The weary fans who have waited all night are rewarded for their patience as the band sign autographs and pose for photos.

4TH FEBRUARY 2008.
TOP LEFT: The pyrotechnic team arrive at the Burswood Dome to rehearse the many explosions and fire effects for the Australian shows. Due to strict aviation regulations travelling with pyrotechnics on board ED FORCE ONE is prohibited. The Pyro team will travel independently to each venue.

LEFT: Bruce in the dressing room, Perth.

BELOW: All members of the band are present to run through all the Pyro cues to avoid incineration during the show. The band then take time to pose with Eddie.

4TH FEBRUARY 2008. Burswood Dome, Perth, Australia.

Janick and Bruce make their way to the stage for the first of two sold out shows in Melbourne.

8TH FEBRUARY 2008. Steve Harris, Sydney Harbour, Australia.

9TH FEBRUARY 2008. Acer Arena, Sydney, Australia.

9TH FEBRUARY 2008. Acer Arena, Sydney, Australia.

11TH FEBRUARY 2008, SYDNEY. Janick is searched before boarding ED FORCE ONE for the short flight to Brisbane.

ED FORCE ONE arrives in Brisbane

12TH FEBRUARY 2008. Entertainment Centre, Brisbane, Australia.

12TH FEBRUARY 2008. Entertainment Centre, Brisbane, Australia.

ABOVE: To celebrate Dickie Bell's impending retirement a crew shot is hastily arranged on stage at the Brisbane Entertainment Centre. A framed picture of the crew will be presented to Dickie in Tokyo.

LEFT: Dickie Bell has been IRON MAIDEN's production manager since 1981 and is credited for keeping the show on the road for all those years. This is his third retirement and he is insistent that this time it is for good. Some say he rules with a rod of Iron; whatever you do, 'take your hands out of your pockets!'

Bruce shows off his DIY haircut.

Steve en route to the stage.

本堂落慶50周年記念開帳 平成20年10月15日〜11月16日

ABOVE: Steve Harris by the 'Thunder Gate', Sensoji Temple, Tokyo.

RIGHT: Dickie Bell walks Adrian Smith to the stage at Tokyo's Messe Hall. After 27 years of dedicated service, this will be the last time Dickie tours with Maiden. Or will it?

Messe Arena, Tokyo. IRON MAIDEN take to the stage at 7:30pm. It is normal for concerts in Japan to start early. What is not customary are venues without seats. The crowd and IRON MAIDEN both benefit from this.

Flight 666 takes off at 1pm Sunday from Tokyo to Los Angeles. Flying via Alaska for United States immigration and a fuel stop. TOP: Bruce takes over the controls for the 5 hour night flight, crossing the International Date line en route to Los Angeles. BOTTOM: Steve Harris, Alaska. On arrival in LA the local time is now 9.30am – some 3 and a half hours back in time and it is still Sunday. Manager Rod Smallwood has a 48 hour birthday.

In honour of the LA Lakers' former home ground, Eddie walks out in front of a capacity crowd sporting the team's colours.

19TH FEBRUARY 2008. The Forum, Los Angeles, CA, USA.

Nicko, backstage warm up.

Adrian honours Mexico.

ABOVE: Janick and Nicko at the Pyramid of the sun.

Close to Mexico City the band visit the pyramids of Teotihuacan. These impressive structures celebrate the sun and the moon and are believed to date back over 2000 years. The surrounding ancient city was populated by over 200,000 people who mysteriously disappeared. Legend has it that inside the pyramids human sacrifice was regularly performed to ensure the sun would continue to rise.

RIGHT: A local guide conducts an ancient ceremony to bless the group and Nicko reciprocates with a prayer of goodwill.

Janick and Nicko are then led deep down into the core of the pyramid under the Altar of Death where, according to local legend, 30,000 people were sacrificed in one day to the Sun God.

23RD FEBRUARY 2008. On arrival in Mexico City the band attend a press conference in the hotel.

ABOVE: The group are led through a staff passageway, past the kitchens and through a single door where the media are waiting.

24TH FEBRUARY 2008. Over 55,000 people are packed into a sold out Foro Sol Stadium, Mexico's National Baseball Stadium.

The crowd is deafening throughout and as a sign of acknowledgement Bruce pauses and lets them sing on.

On departure, an important piece of paperwork goes astray by the local Airport authority leading to a real 'Mexican Stand Off'.
FAR RIGHT: Relief Pilot Ivan is ordered by air traffic control to abort take-off and return the aircraft to the gate. ED FORCE ONE powers down on the taxi way between the runway and the terminal, preventing any plane access to or from the terminal. A major delay now would jeopardise tomorrow's show in Costa Rica.

A precarious situation develops between flight crew and the authorities. Tensions begin to rise and language difficulties add to the drama.

LEFT: Captain John Mahon finally receives the 'important' flight documentation allowing ED FORCE ONE to depart. Flight 666 takes off 90 minutes late, Mexico City airport re-opens and ED FORCE ONE touches down in San Jose in time for the stage equipment to clear customs.

All tickets for the show sold out over 3 months ago and the excitement in San Jose builds. To relax before the show, Nicko sets off for a round of golf. Having only played one hole, a golf ball fires past, striking Nicko on the left forearm; causing a possible fracture. Medics attend to the arm as bruising appears and it begins to swell. Nicko rests the arm, covers it with an ice pack and a call is made to the production office at the venue, warning Nicko has been injured.

The crew await news as Nicko is taken to hospital and the swollen arm is x-rayed.

A capacity crowd at the Estadio Ricardo Saprissa stadium.

ABOVE: One hour before show time Nicko arrives. The arm is not fractured and although painful, Nicko is able to play the show.

IRON MAIDEN smash the record in Costa Rica for the biggest crowd attendance ever for a music event in this country.

26TH FEBRUARY 2008. Saprissa Stadium, San Jose, Costa Rica.

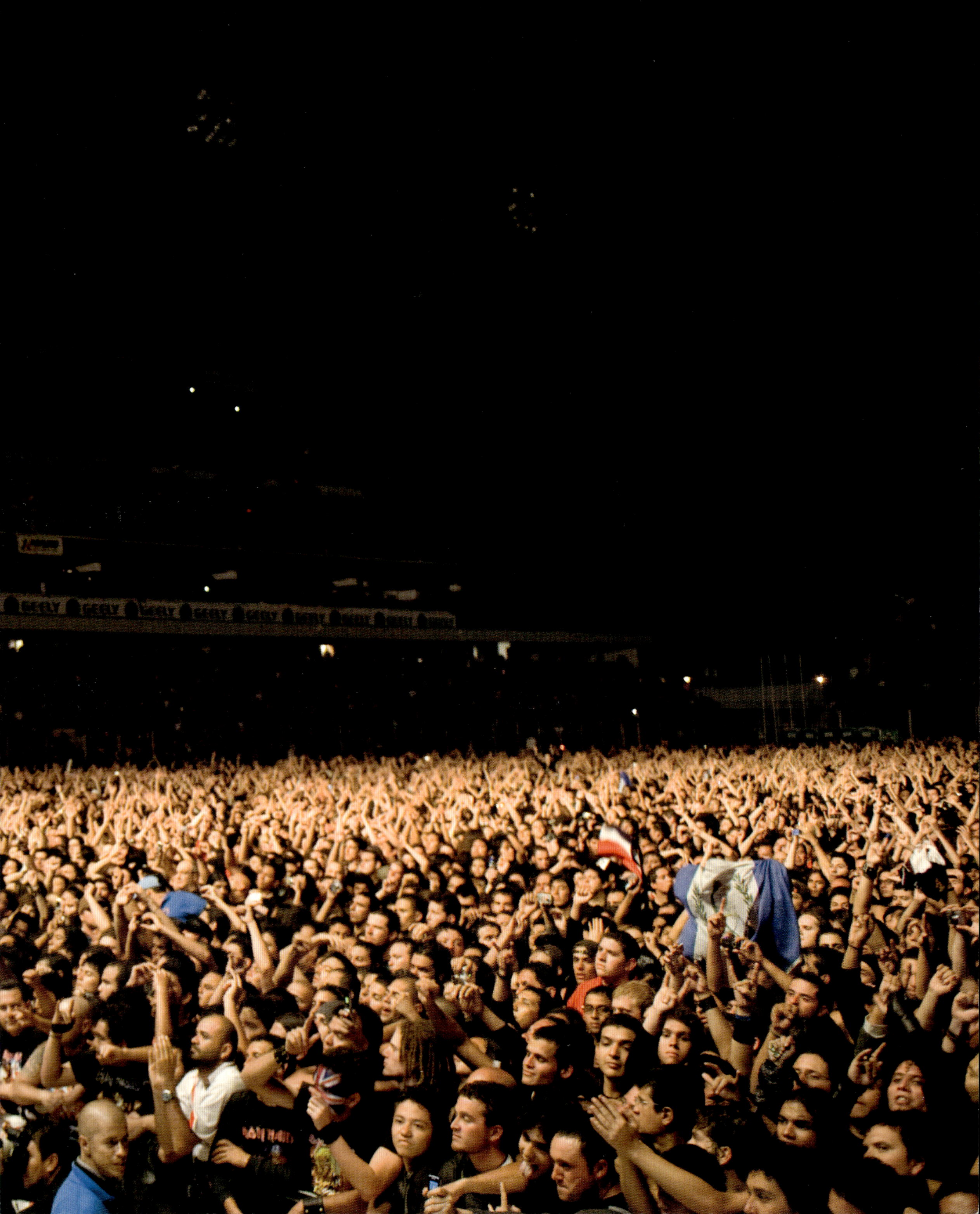

The scene in Bogota airport is complete chaos as the members of IRON MAIDEN make their way into the terminal. It is unclear which way to turn as the band are led through one check point after another. Finally they are led into the President's private immigration area where the military and police all want autographs. A dozen police outriders escort the band through the city and around the Simon Bolivar Park where mile upon mile of tents line the road. Fans started queuing for the show over a week ago. This is Maiden's first visit to Bogota and by show day there are 45,000 people waiting to welcome them.

ABOVE: The crowd unveil a 100 foot Maiden Colombian flag which stretches out over the audience.

Two bars into 'The Number Of The Beast' the Maiden crew smell electrical burning and Bruce struggles to clear his throat on stage. The crew investigate and discover a cloud of tear gas is blowing across the venue from the outside park. This along with water cannons are being used by the militia to deter the many fans without tickets trying to break into the sold out show.

IRON MAIDEN play on and the tear gas clears.

ABOVE: The day before a sold out show at the 40,000 capacity Palmiers Stadium, Steve meets up with his team mates from IRON MAIDEN FC at the Sao Paulo Atletico sports ground. Based in the East End of London, the team have flown out to play a squad hastily pulled together of ex Corinthians, members of Sepultura and music execs. Within the first 15 minutes, Maiden FC are 2 goals ahead. After a full 90 minutes of play in blistering heat the final score is IRON MAIDEN 8 – BRAZIL 0.

RIGHT: Band Manager Rod Smallwood lends his support.

2ND MARCH 2008.
ABOVE: IRON MAIDEN win the football but the crowd in Sao Paulo claim victory for being the loudest and the most enthusiastic of the tour so far.

LEFT: Bruce draped in a Brazilian flag stops the show as a chant of 'Ole Ole Ole' erupts from the stadium.

4TH MARCH 2008. The military police hold back fans as the band arrive at Curitiba Airport.

RIGHT: Bruce powers down ED FORCE ONE and jumps aboard the people carrier that is transporting the band to their hotel.

ABOVE: As the vehicle drives onto the perimeter road, crowds flood out from the main terminal and give chase. Police outriders clear a path through the airport gates and the vehicle exits onto the streets of Buenos Aires.

With the crowds left behind, everyone relaxes and enjoys a few minutes of temporary calm until the cavalcade turns the last corner towards the hotel. Although extra security have been drafted in, the vehicle is suddenly surrounded by hordes of fans. It is virtually impossible to enter the hotel. The band are weary after a long day of travel but are still in good spirits and acknowledge the fans as they are escorted into the hotel.

The security withdraw and secure the doors as the high spirited crowd surges forward singing 'Run To The Hills'.

LEFT: The hotel manager, fearing the glass may shatter any moment, moves all guests to a safe distance and pleads for calm.

RIGHT: From either side of ED FORCE ONE, the snow capped peaks of the Andes can be seen stretching out as far as the horizon. Almost everyone on board is taking in the view.

On the ground fans have been gathering for several hours and as Bruce taxis ED FORCE ONE to its stand it is clear that this arrival is going to be a lively one. BELOW: All along the perimeter fence there are masses of fans waving flags and chanting "Maiden". As the band are quickly escorted through Immigration the legions of fans move along the outer walls and pause at every window desperate to get a glimpse.

This continues all the way through the terminal until everyone is bundled into vehicles and escorted away from the chaos. The hotel is no different and security advise entry via the underground staff entrance to avoid a repeat of Buenos Aires.

ABOVE: Once inside the hotel the band have a very brief break and are then whisked in front of Chile's media for a press conference. Outside, the hotel is surrounded by cheering fans.

LEFT: Later that evening the band relax for a meal and sample Chile's fine wines with predictable results.

ABOVE: High above Santiago on the edge of the Andes, Steve Harris shows the Flight 666 film crew, Kevin, Martin, Sam and Scot, exactly what they can do with their sound equipment.

RIGHT: As the film crew attempt a piece to camera, Steve notices something orange with 8 legs moving closer. The tarantula spider crosses the road with a little help from Steve.

LEFT: Steve and Nicko make their way to the stage in Santiago.

9TH MARCH 2008. Pista Atletica, Santiago, Chile

9TH MARCH 2008. Pista Atletica, Santiago, Chile.

ABOVE: Day of show and the entire stage set has been built, lighting and sound rigs in place but no power. The Maiden sound rig requires UK 220 volts and the brand new San Juan Coliseum can only offer US 110 volts. Technical details for the show were sent months in advance and an essential transformer is not supplied. As the venue staff search Puerto Rico for a transformer electricians try and resolve the problem. It is looking very likely the show will have to be cancelled. 12,000 people are waiting patiently outside for the doors to open. FAR RIGHT: At 6.15pm, Rod Smallwood films a piece to camera in front of the IRON MAIDEN stage set. If the show is cancelled, the film will be given to the local TV news so the fans get an explanation – it would not be possible to reschedule. RIGHT: The Maiden road crew can do nothing but continue to await news. As the venue prepares to cancel, the electricians 'hotwire' the generator giving a stable 220 volt current. It works and the doors open.

The stage gets power and IRON MAIDEN take to the stage on time.

Laura Ingle from Fox News interviews Nicko in flight.

Dave Murray leaves the dressing room in New Jersey.

Travelling over 50,000 miles across 5 continents, 23 shows in only 45 days and playing to nearly 500,000 fans, the first leg of this successful tour comes to a close in Toronto. It is a world first for any band to tour in this way and everyone backstage is in a joyous mood as IRON MAIDEN take to the stage.

Onstage, Bruce thanks the Killer Krew and everyone involved with ED FORCE ONE for all their hard work.

The very next day the band board ED FORCE ONE and head home to Stansted, London. Job done!

BOTTOM LEFT: An exhausted but happy crew prepare for the final flight.

BELOW: Jeremy Smith from ROCK-IT CARGO loads the band's precious freight for the very last time on this tour.

SOMEWHERE BACK IN TIME
WORLD TOUR 2008

FEATURING HIGHLIGHTS FROM THE SECOND LEG ACROSS NORTH AMERICA

MAY 2008
21ST SAN ANTONIO, TX, USA
22ND HOUSTON, TX, USA
25TH ALBUQUERQUE, NM, USA
26TH PHOENIX, AZ, USA
28TH CONCORD, CA, USA
30TH LOS ANGELES, CA, USA
31ST LOS ANGELES, CA, USA

JUNE 2008
2ND SEATTLE, WA, USA
3RD VANCOUVER, BC, CANADA

5TH CALGARY, AB, CANADA
6TH EDMONTON, AB, CANADA
8TH REGINA, SK, CANADA
9TH WINNIPEG, SK, CANADA
11TH ROSEMONT IL, USA
12TH CUYAHOGA FALLS, OH, USA
14TH HOLMDEL, NJ, USA
15TH NEW YORK, NY, USA
17TH CAMDEN, NJ, USA
18TH COLUMBIA, MD, USA
20TH MANSFIELD, MA, USA
21ST MONTREAL, QC, CANADA

22ND MAY 2008. Woodlands, Houston, Texas, USA.

25TH MAY 2008. Journal Pavilion, Albuquerque, New Mexico, USA.

26TH MAY 2008. Cricket Pavilion, Phoenix, USA.

SOMEWHERE BACK IN TIME
WORLD TOUR 2008

FEATURING HIGHLIGHTS FROM THE THIRD LEG ACROSS EUROPE

JUNE 2008
27TH BOLOGNA, ITALY
29TH DESSEL, BELGIUM

JULY 2008
1ST PARIS, FRANCE
2ND PARIS, FRANCE
5TH TWICKENHAM, LONDON, UK
9TH LISBON, PORTUGAL
11TH MERIDA, SPAIN
16TH STOCKHOLM, SWEDEN
18TH HELSINKI, FINLAND
19TH TAMPERE, FINLAND
22ND TRONDHEIM, NORWAY
24TH OSLO, NORWAY

26TH GOTHENBURG, SWEDEN
27TH HORSENS, DENMARK
31ST WACKEN FESTIVAL, GERMANY

AUGUST 2008
2ND ATHENS, GREECE
4TH BUCHAREST, ROMANIA
7TH WARSAW, POLAND
8TH PRAGUE, CZECH REP
10TH SPLIT, CROATIA
12TH BUDAPEST, HUNGARY
14TH BASEL, SWITZERLAND
16TH ASSEN, NETHERLANDS
19TH MOSCOW, RUSSIA

ABOVE: Earlier in the day Janick surveys the giant stadium.

RIGHT: The band prepare to go on stage at the home of English rugby.

LEFT: Maiden security chief, Jeff Weir, arrives to escort the band up to the stage.

IRON MAIDEN make a triumphant return to the UK playing to 50,000 fans at Twickenham stadium.

5TH JULY 2008. Twickenham Stadium, London, England.

RIGHT:
Steve and Janick before walking out in front of 57,000 people at Ullevi stadium in Gothenburg.

This is the second time Maiden have sold out the National Stadium and Gothenburg is transformed into 'Maidenville' by the hordes of devoted Swedish fans.

26TH JULY 2008. Ullevi Stadium, Gothenburg, Sweden.

SOMEWHERE BACK IN TIME WORLD TOUR 2009

FEATURING HIGHLIGHTS FROM THE FOURTH LEG ON BOARD ED FORCE ONE

FEBRUARY 2009
10TH BELGRADE, SERBIA
13TH DUBAI, UAE
15TH BANGALORE, INDIA
20TH AUCKLAND, NEW ZEALAND
22ND CHRISTCHURCH, NEW ZEALAND
25TH MONTERREY, MEXICO
26TH GUADALAJARA, MEXICO
28TH MEXICO CITY, MEXICO

MARCH 2009
3RD SAN JOSE, COSTA RICA
5TH CARACAS, VENEZUELA
7TH BOGOTA, COLOMBIA

10TH QUITO, ECUADOR
12TH MANAUS, BRAZIL
14TH RIO DE JANEIRO, BRAZIL
15TH SAO PAULO, BRAZIL
18TH BELO HORIZONTE, BRAZIL
20TH BRASILIA, BRAZIL
22ND SANTIAGO, CHILE
26TH LIMA, PERU
28TH BUENOS AIRES, ARGENTINA
31ST RECIFE, BRAZIL

APRIL 2009
2ND FT LAUDERDALE, FLORIDA, USA

Guitars, drums, staging, drapes, sound & lighting desks, backline and Eddie all have to be loaded into ED FORCE ONE's customised cargo bay after each show. Everything has to be loaded on to specially designed flight pallets, covered in a protective fire blanket and securely strapped down before each flight. The entire process takes up to 6 hours and another 3 to unload.

To keep ED FORCE ONE in the air, two engineers travel with the touring party to carry out routine maintenance after each and every flight. Any defects on the aircraft noted by the Flight Crew can be attended to before the next departure.

It is rare for a major music act to visit Quito and unprecedented for a stage show as ambitious as IRON MAIDEN's to drop in. At 9200ft above sea level it is one of the highest cities in the world. Maiden arrive 2 days before show day in order to acclimatise to the altitude. On the streets surrounding the airport over 1500 fans are desperate to get closer to Maiden. The first attempt to drive out is aborted after advice from the military, who are struggling to secure the perimeter. Maiden finally escape by sending the Killer Krew to an alternative gate as a decoy. At the hotel, police link arms to hold back the enthusiastic crowd that is growing ever larger. Fans unfurl a large banner welcoming Maiden to Ecuador. High on a distant hill on the outskirts of the city massive letters spell out 'Maiden'.

FAR LEFT: Nicko at the Equator. 0-0-0 Latitude – this is the middle of the world.

ABOVE: Nicko hits a golf ball from the Northern hemisphere into the Southern hemisphere.

LEFT: Steve Harris high above Quito city.

BELOW: Bruce challenges Ecuador's Olympic team to a series of duels.

Situated at the basin of the Amazon and deep in the rain forest, Maiden are invited on a boat to see where the Amazon river begins.

ABOVE: The cruise leaves the quay in beautiful sunshine which soon fades as threatening black clouds move in and the rain pours. The River Solimões, a dark clear water, meets the muddy Rio Negre creating a stark line in the water.

FAR RIGHT: Janick and Nicko stand in the rain at the confluence.

LEFT: Adrian Smith hangs on as the boat turns around to return to Manaus.

BELOW: Nicko McBrain, 12th March 2009, Sambodrome Stadium, Manaus, Brazil.

ABOVE: ED FORCE ONE touches down in Rio for the premiere of the movie 'FLIGHT 666'.

RIGHT: The band arrive at the prestigious Cine Odeon to rapturous applause and a media frenzy begins.

ABOVE: The band line up in front of the world's press.

LEFT: Bruce introduces the movie to the audience before discreetly leaving the theatre.

The movie receives critical acclaim and goes on to win 'Best Music Documentary' at the South By South West Music awards in Texas and a Juno award (Canadian equivalent of a Grammy) for Best Music DVD.

Despite torrential rain hindering the stage build the previous day, the show in Rio is faultless.

Flight 666 from Rio is put back to 2pm to allow Bruce a full night of sleep after the previous night's show. Without this rest period, strict aviation rules would prohibit Bruce piloting that day. The Killer Krew travel by road overnight and start the set build at 7am at the renowned Formula 1 racing circuit Interlagos.

As the band prepare to take to the stage at 8pm there are still 20,000 excited ticket holders queuing outside. The band and Manager Rod Smallwood, insist it would not be appropriate to start the show and delay the stage time. To avoid the crowd getting restless, Rod Smallwood makes an announcement from the stage to rapturous applause. By 9pm there are 70,000 people inside the stadium chanting "Maiden" and the band go on. The reaction from the crowd is euphoric.

LEFT: The day after the show Bruce rides a helicopter back to the Interlagos track and takes control of a supercharged Porsche 911. After several hair raising laps around the circuit (one with a terrified journalist from *The Times* newspaper), Bruce challenges the attending media to a Go-Kart race on the training circuit. 25 brutally fast laps around the 'mini-Interlagos' track later and Bruce comes in first place, winning a gold watch that runs backwards in time.

LEFT: Following a morning of racing cars, Bruce fences Brazil's finest athletes for the next 3 hours!

17TH MARCH 2009. Sao Paulo, Brazil.

High above the stage set riggers secure the massive light show.

Santiago 2008 sold out instantly and the demand for tickets was unprecedented. As promised Maiden return, but this time with the full stage show flown down by air freight from Sao Paulo. To avoid any disappointment the Club Hipico Racecourse has double the capacity of 2008.

RIGHT: Bruce relaxes backstage before stepping out in front of 60,000+ in Chile.

BELOW: As Maiden take to the stage, a small minority jump over the barriers and refuse to move. Security attempt to clear them without success and the Carabineros, Chile's much revered riot police, step into the pit area with full armour and batons. Fortunately just the sight of the Carabineros is enough to move the offenders away without the use of force. The show continues without incident.

1ST APRIL 2009. ED FORCE ONE band and crew take time for a group photo on a fuel stop in Barbados.

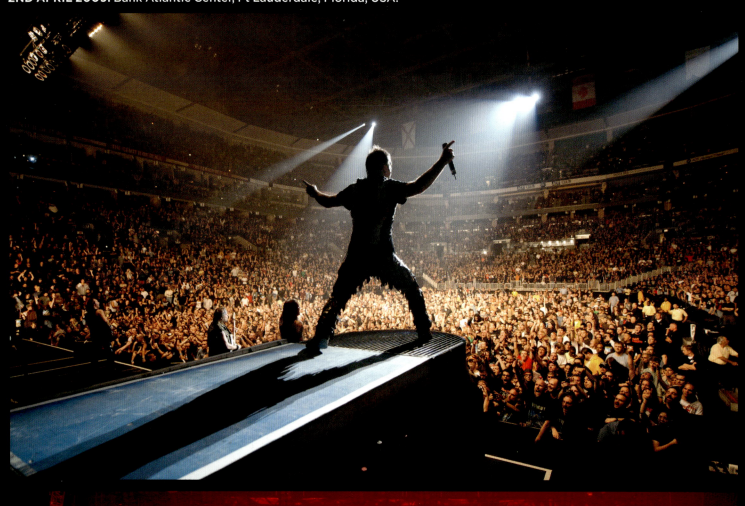

2ND APRIL 2009. Ft Lauderdale, Florida.
IRON MAIDEN play the final show on the Somewhere Back In Time tour.
Travelling by air, land and sea across 5 continents, 38 countries and reaching
over 2 million fans, the Somewhere Back in Time tour is complete.

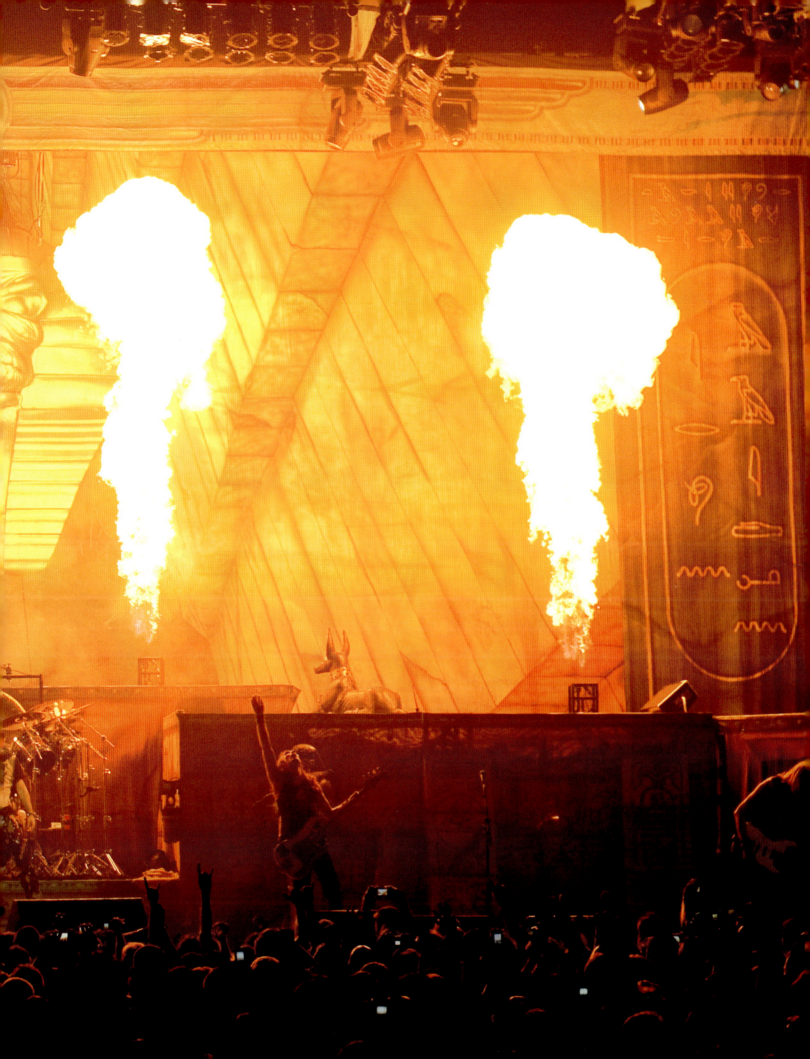

THE KILLER KREW

Tour Manager: Ian Day

Tour Manager: Steve Gadd

Production Manager: Patrick Ledwith

Lighting Designer: Rob Coleman

Production Coordinator: Zeb Minto

Monitor Engineer: Steve 'Gonzo' Smith

Stage Manager: Bill Conte

FOH Sound Engineer: Doug Hall

Guitar Techs: Colin Price, Justin Garrick, Sean Brady & Michael Kenney (& keyboards).

Drum Tech: Charlie Charlesworth

Sound Tech: Ian 'Squid' Walsh

Set Carpenters: Paul Stratford, Ashley Groom, Philip Stewart & Griff Dickinson

Sound System Tech: Mike Hackman

Lighting Chief: Antti Saari

Video Director: Andy Matthews

Wardrobe: Natasha De Sampayo

Head of Security: Jeffrey Weir

Masseuse/Security: Peter Lokrantz

Video Tech: Nicholas Birtwistle

Production Assistant: Kerry Harris

THE FINAL FRONTIER WORLD TOUR 2010

FEATURING HIGHLIGHTS FROM NORTH AMERICA AND EUROPE

JUNE 2010
9TH DALLAS, TX, USA
11TH HOUSTON, TX, USA
12TH SAN ANTONIO, TX, USA
14TH DENVER, CO, USA
16TH ALBUQUERQUE, NM, USA
17TH PHOENIX, AZ, USA
19TH SAN BERNARDINO, CA, USA
20TH CONCORD, CA, USA
22ND AUBURN, WA, USA
24TH VANCOUVER, BC, CANADA
26TH EDMONTON, AB, CANADA
27TH CALGARY, AB, CANADA
29TH SASKATOON, SK, CANADA
30TH WINNIPEG, MB, CANADA

JULY 2010
3RD TORONTO, ON, CANADA
6TH OTTAWA, ON, CANADA
7TH MONTREAL, QC, CANADA
9TH QUEBEC CITY, CANADA

11TH HOLMDEL, NJ, USA
12TH NEW YORK, NY, USA
14TH PITTSBURGH, PA, USA
15TH CLEVELAND, OH, USA
17TH DETROIT, MI, USA
18TH CHICAGO, IL, USA
20TH WASHINGTON D.C., USA

30TH DUBLIN, IRELAND

AUGUST 2010
1ST KNEBWORTH, UK
5TH WACKEN, GERMANY
7TH STOCKHOLM, SWEDEN
8TH PORI, FINLAND
11TH BERGEN, NORWAY
14TH BUDAPEST, HUNGARY
15TH TRANSYLVANIA, ROMANIA
17TH UDINE, ITALY
19TH HASSELT, BELGIUM
21ST VALENCIA, SPAIN

In a rehearsal studio in Ft Lauderdale IRON MAIDEN run through the set list for The Final Frontier 2010 tour.

The tour kicks off in Dallas in 4 days' time. The production team and set designers (Hangman) are there already, building the new stage set in anticipation of the band's arrival.

ABOVE: Bruce Dickinson arrives at the venue to inspect the new stage set.

ABOVE RIGHT: The Final Frontier Eddie is unveiled.

RIGHT: Soundcheck in Dallas.

Production rehearsals continue for a second day and go on until late at night. This leg of the tour will use trucks and tour buses to transport the show and crew across North America. The band will travel to each city using a Gulf Stream Jet and Bruce will occasionally use the 'Bruce Goose' (a 7 seated twin prop aircraft) to get to shows.

US Navy Commander 'Patton' Thurman and Major Marc 'Monkey' Mulkey take Bruce and Rod to
'Carswell Field' Naval base to inspect the F/A 18 Hornets up close and try out the flight simulators.

In celebration of the band's soon to be released studio album *The Final Frontier*, IRON MAIDEN are invited on a VIP tour of NASA Houston.

ABOVE & RIGHT: The band are shown around Space Shuttle and the International Space Station training unit by esteemed astronaut Mike Massimino.

BELOW MIDDLE: Mike gives the band a personal tour of NASA, recounting his own first hand experiences in space.

BELOW: Nicko on the Space Shuttle lavatory.

ABOVE: The band are then taken into the live NASA Mission Control Center.

ABOVE LEFT: Janick and Dave take in the atmosphere of the historic moon landings operations room.

ABOVE: Nicko and Rod on the hot phone.

The tour continues into the evening and Bruce, Nicko, Dave and Janick are offered the chance to fly the Space Shuttle flight simulator (an experience that is normally reserved for astronauts only). Everyone is strapped tightly into the flight seats and the cockpit is tilted back to simulate a real launch. Bruce is at the controls first, blasting off with the entire cockpit shaking. The cockpit rolls over and the trainer informs Bruce he is travelling at 17,000mph. The booster rockets are ejected and out of the windows the world fades further away. After entering orbit Bruce re-enters the earth's atmosphere and takes full control, gliding the Space Shuttle home successfully using a projected guidance system. Everyone takes a turn blasting off and the engineer congratulates Nicko for a 'text book' landing.

Tres Amigos. The Alamo, San Antonio, Texas.

Adrian Smith, Denver, Colorado.

TOP LEFT: THE 'Bruce Goose' is fuelled up at a Santa Monica Airfield.

TOP RIGHT: For fun, Bruce races the band party to Concord; flying out of Santa Monica an hour earlier than the rest of the band in their Gulf Stream Jet.

ABOVE: Bruce lands 20 minutes ahead of the group much to the band's amusement.

24TH JUNE 2010. Vancouver, Canada.

The Final Frontier. IRON MAIDEN's 15th studio album is released on 13th August 2010 to critical acclaim. The album reaches No.1 in over 28 countries.

THE FINAL FRONTIER WORLD TOUR 2011

FEATURING HIGHLIGHTS FROM THE THIRD LEG 'AROUND THE WORLD IN 66 DAYS'

FEBRUARY 2011
11TH MOSCOW, RUSSIA
15TH SINGAPORE
17TH JAKARTA, INDONESIA
20TH BALI, INDONESIA
23RD MELBOURNE, AUSTRALIA
24TH SYDNEY, AUSTRALIA
26TH BRISBANE, AUSTRALIA
27TH SYDNEY, AUSTRALIA

MARCH 2011
4TH MELBOURNE, AUSTRALIA
5TH ADELAIDE, AUSTRALIA
7TH SOUNDWAVE, PERTH, AUSTRALIA
10TH SEOUL, SOUTH KOREA
12TH TOKYO, JAPAN*
13TH TOKYO, JAPAN*
17TH MONTERREY, MEXICO

18TH MEXICO CITY, MEXICO
20TH BOGOTA, COLOMBIA
23RD LIMA, PERU
26TH SAO PAULO, BRAZIL
28TH RIO DE JANEIRO, BRAZIL
30TH BRASILIA, BRAZIL

*CANCELLED DUE TO EARTHQUAKE

APRIL 2011
1ST BELEM, BRAZIL
3RD RECIFE, BRAZIL
5TH CURITIBA, BRAZIL
8TH BUENOS AIRES, ARGENTINA
10TH SANTIAGO, CHILE
14TH SAN JUAN, PUERTO RICO
16TH FT LAUDERDALE, FLORIDA, USA
17TH TAMPA, FLORIDA, USA

The new Final Frontier ED FORCE ONE is prepared for the 2011 world tour.

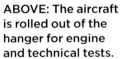

ABOVE: The aircraft is rolled out of the hanger for engine and technical tests.

LEFT: Bruce inspects the aircraft 48 hours before departure.

ABOVE: Minutes before ED FORCE ONE takes to the skies Bruce is alerted to a possible malfunction of the left wing de-icer mechanism. BELOW: The band and crew are forced to stand down while the possible cause is investigated.

Engineers scramble all over the aircraft and locate the problem. Although a minor fault, it has to be fixed. ABOVE: Janick holds the offending part. Contingency plans are put in place to unload the aircraft, then use a freighter to transport the equipment to Moscow and fly the band and crew on an alternative aircraft. Thankfully it doesn't come to this.

The faulty part is quickly replaced and Bruce gets clearance for take off. ABOVE: Dickie Bell rounds up the crew and ED FORCE ONE takes to the skies. The 2011 Final Frontier World tour begins.

On arrival in Moscow, TV crews, oblivious to the sub-zero temperatures, greet IRON MAIDEN with enthusiasm.

OPPOSITE PAGE:
The following morning Steve Harris stops to sign autographs outside the hotel and ventures into Red Square.

INTRO
FINAL FRONTIER
ELDORADO
2 MINUTES
COMING HOME
DANCE OF DEATH
TROOPER
BLOOD BROTHERS
WICKERMAN
WILD WIND BLOWS
EVIL THAT MEN DO
TALISMAN
FEAR OF THE DARK
IRON MAIDEN
————————————————
NUMBER OF BEAST
HALLOWED
RUNNING FREE

The day before the show IRON MAIDEN arrive at the Olympic Stadium for a soundcheck and production rehearsal.

3pm: ED FORCE ONE covered in frost and ice at Moscow Domodedovo Airport. The temperature has plummeted to a biting -20°C.

The aircraft is sprayed with anti-ice fluid before take-off. All de-icer mechanisms on the aircraft are functioning correctly.

Heading South East via Baku the sun rises over Asia. Ground crew at Singapore airport excitedly welcome IRON MAIDEN. The temperature is +32 degrees, a shift of 52 degrees from Moscow.

Adrian Smith looks
out across the skyline
of Singapore from the
26th floor of the band's
hotel. Meanwhile fans
have been gathering
since dawn at the
Indoor Stadium.

15TH FEBRUARY 2011. Singapore Indoor Stadium.

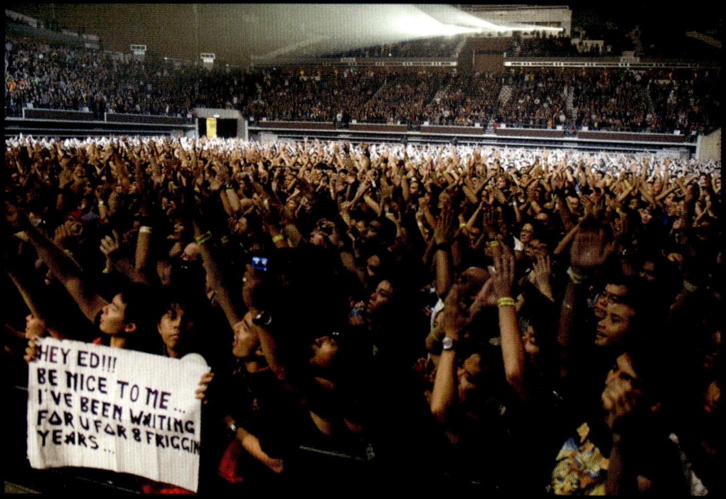

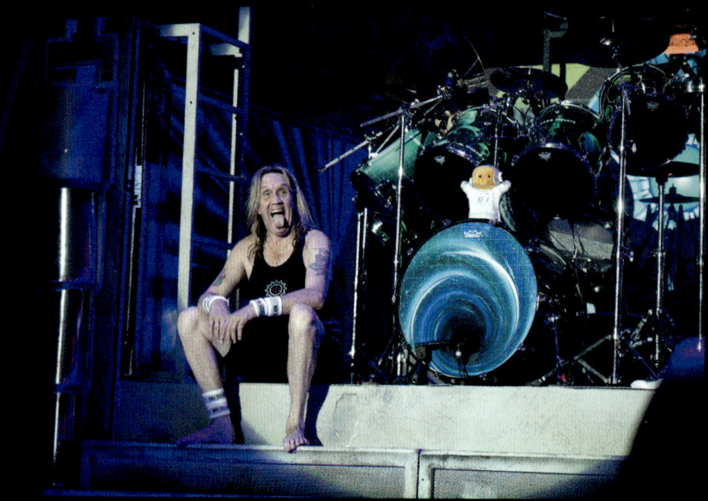

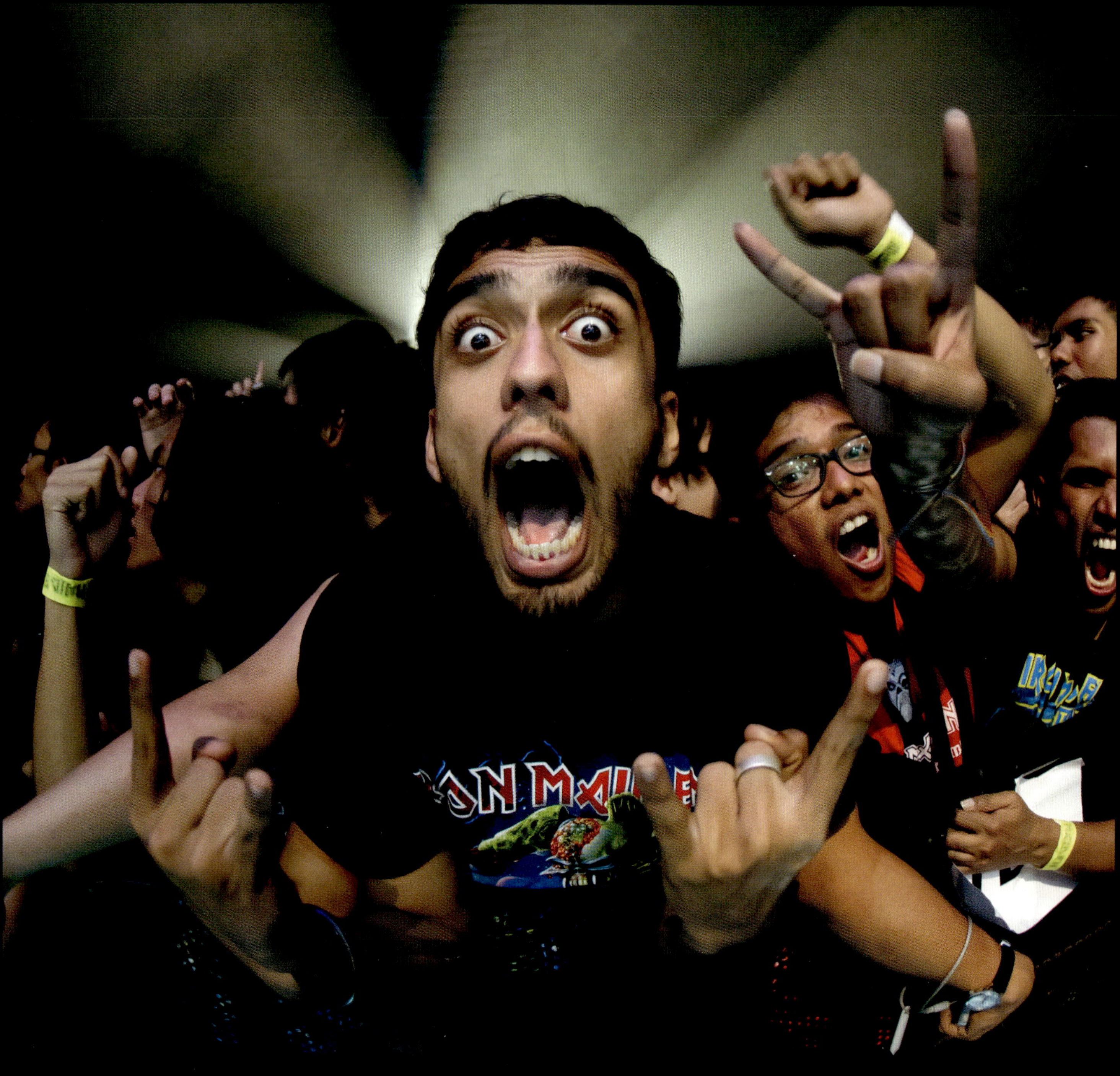

ABOVE: Customs officials board the aircraft on arrival in Jakarta.

ABOVE RIGHT: Airport staff leave their official positions to pose with the group.

RIGHT: Hundreds of fans wait for the band on the other side of the exit doors.

BELOW: IRON MAIDEN are hurried through the lively crowd and into several vehicles.

ABOVE:
Police inspect
the concert site
with sniffer dogs.
No, not drugs,
looking for bombs!

LEFT:
Bruce attends
a busy press
conference for the
waiting Indonesian
media at the hotel.

RIGHT: Outside the venue at Ancol Bay, Muslim IRON MAIDEN fans pray to Allah at a musalla (a mini mosque) before entering the concert. The imam is among those wearing IRON MAIDEN T-shirts.

OPPOSITE TOP: On the outskirts of the concert site, riot police with tear gas and water cannons monitor the crowd waiting to react to the first sign of trouble. There is none.

Bruce returns to the hotel post show and pre-shower.

TOP: Bruce checks the cargo is secure before the short flight to Bali.

RIGHT: Military police clear a route and assist the band's fast getaway from the airport.

BOTTOM LEFT: Hindu Maiden fans follow the cavalcade through the streets of Bali with great excitement.

BOTTOM RIGHT: Nicko and Dave are greeted at the hotel with necklaces made of Frangipani flowers.

The day before the show, Bruce and Janick with assorted family and crew visit the Ulawatu 'Monkey' Temple to witness the legendary Kecak fire dance. TOP LEFT: A choir of seventy Balinese men chant 'cak.cak.cak' as a story of treachery is played out by Balinese dancers. TOP RIGHT: The climatic finale of the fire dance.

ABOVE LEFT: Bruce and Janick with the Kecak dancers.

The Garuda Wisnu Kencana Cultural Park is one of the most unique settings for an IRON MAIDEN concert. ABOVE: Bruce, wearing a gift (the shirt!) from the Balinese promoter, inspects the stage before a spot of rock climbing.

FAR LEFT: Although 'retired', Dickie Bell has helped with much of the logistics for the tour and has flown ahead to Indonesia to guide the local production crew.

LEFT: The giant park gates are opened to the hordes of eager fans.

23RD FEBRUARY 2011. Hisense Arena, Melbourne, Australia.

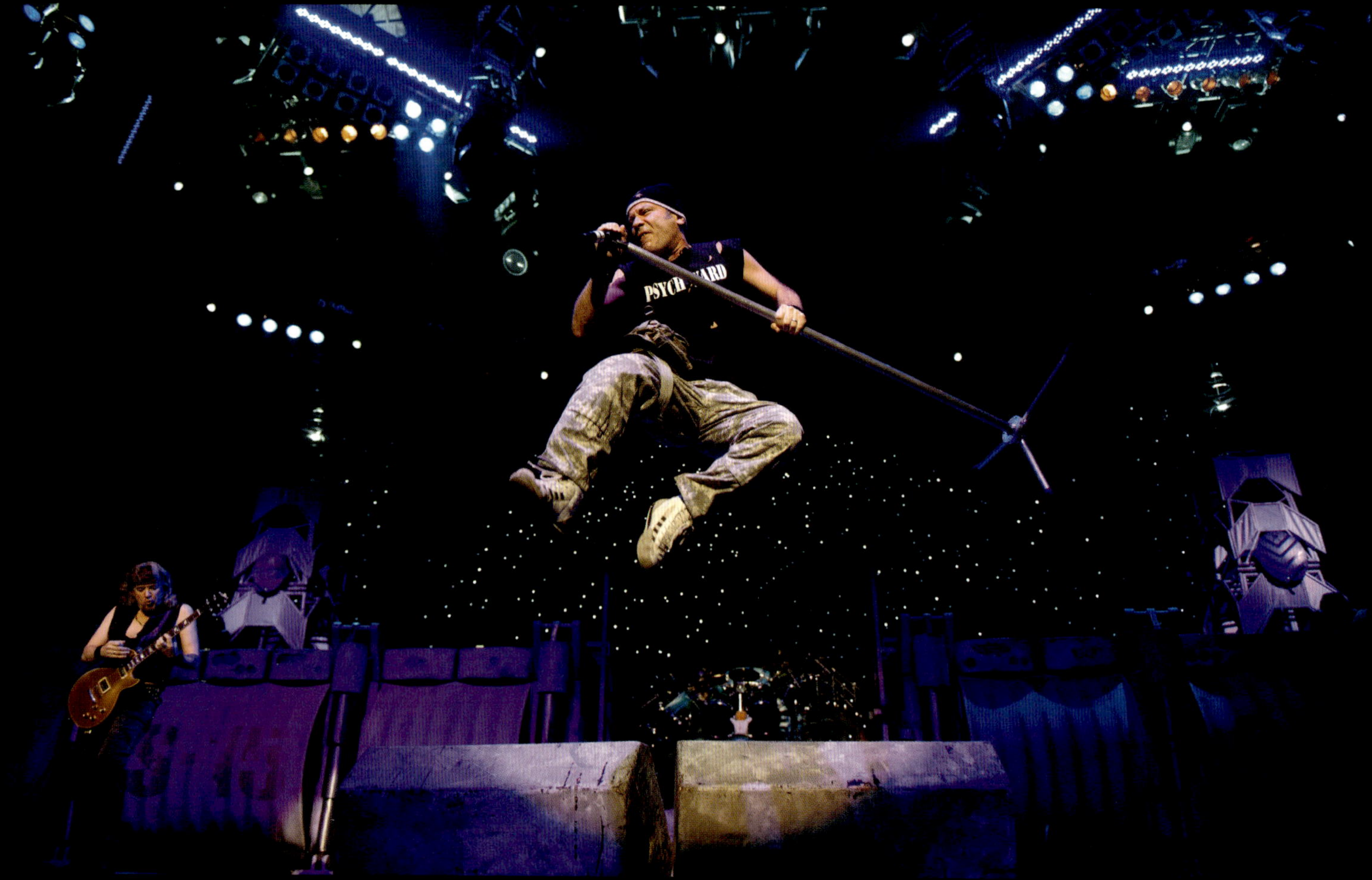

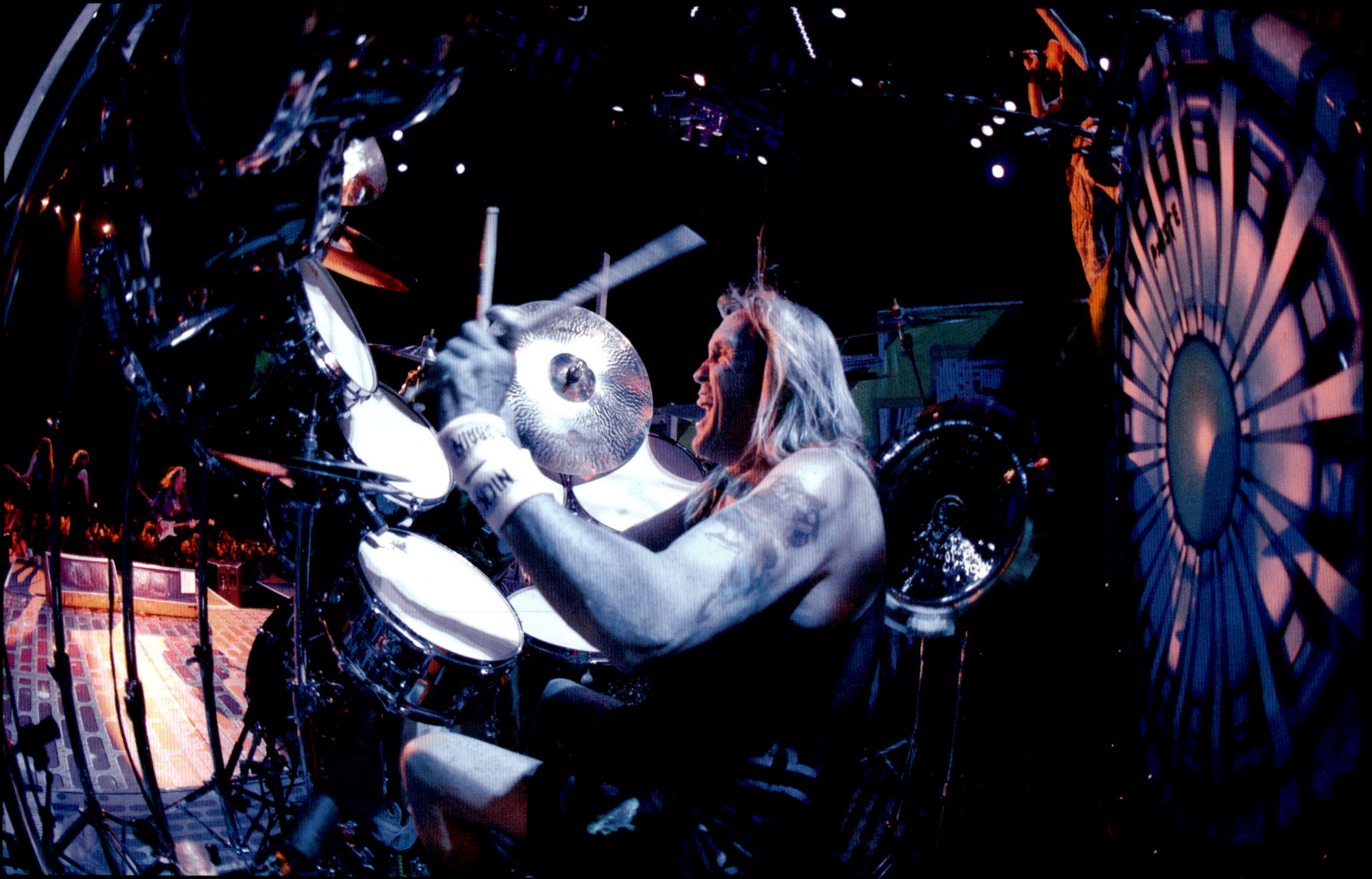

Bruce covers his foot with ice, post show; following a climbing incident a few days earlier in Bali.

En route to Sydney Janick displays a painful 5 inch bruise after landing badly on stage.

24TH FEBRUARY 2011. Sydney, Australia.

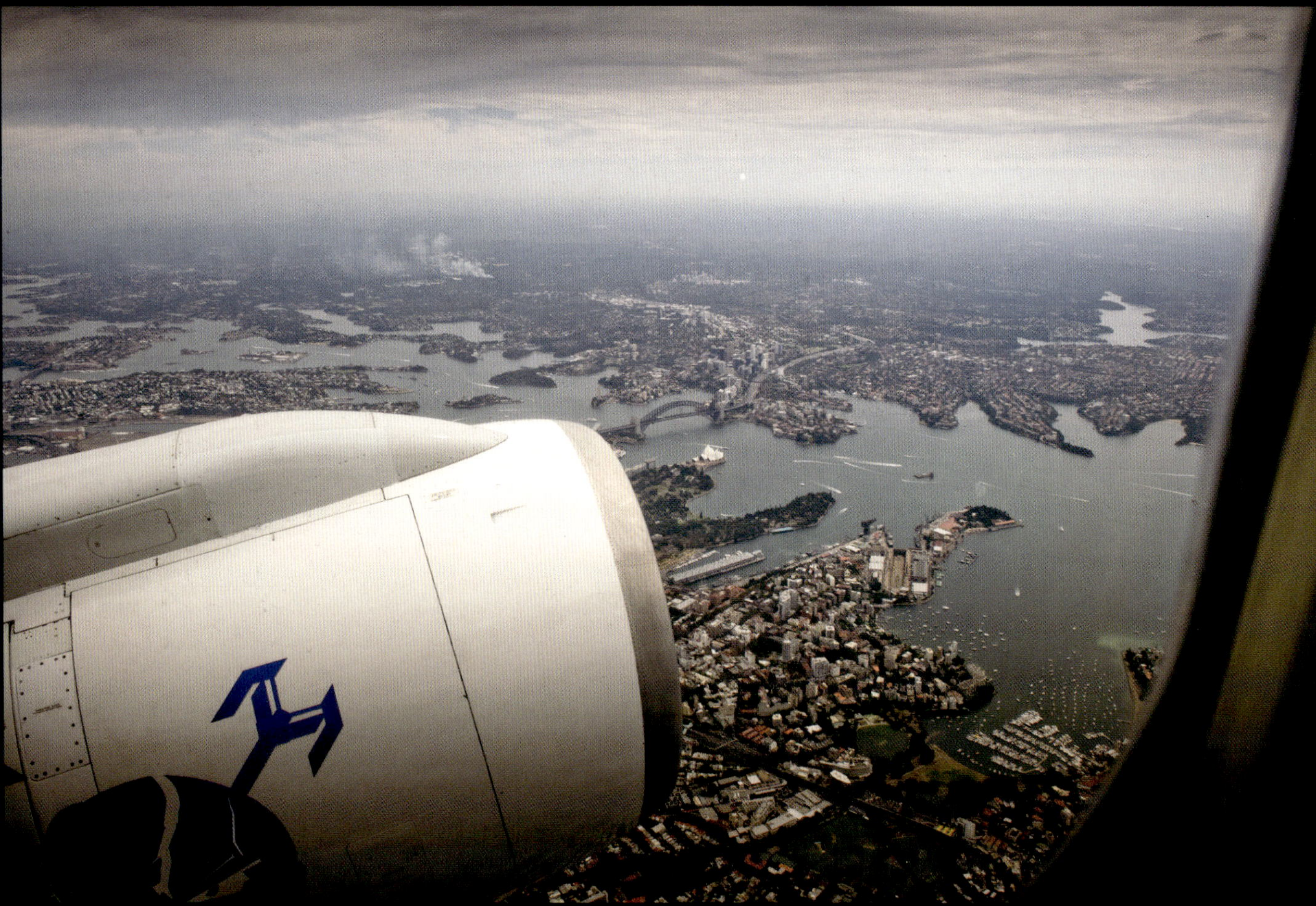

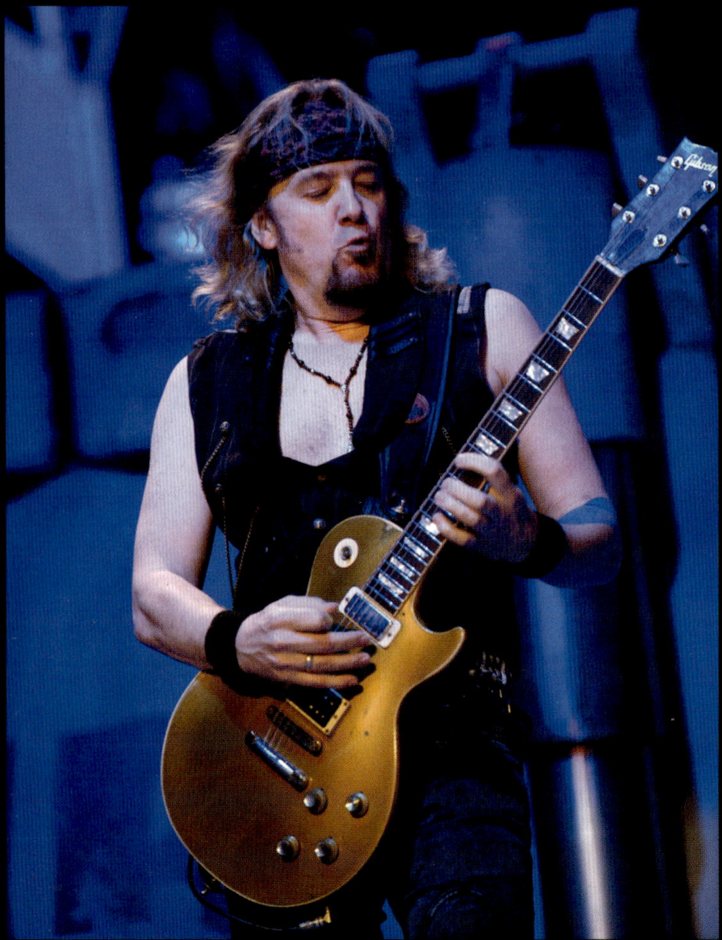

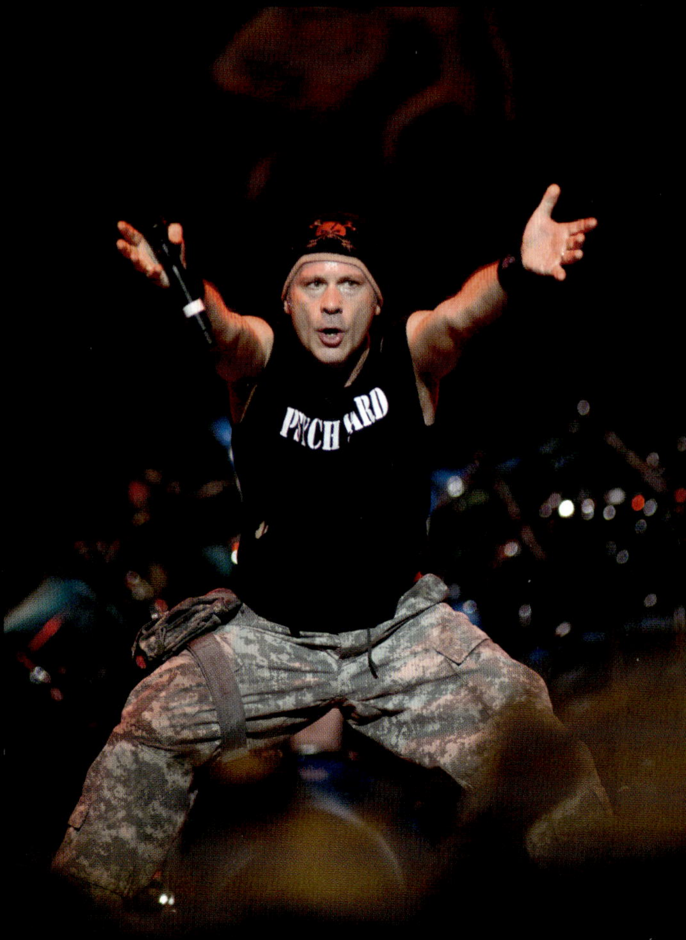

26TH FEBRUARY 2011. Steve Harris at the Lone Pine Koala Sanctuary.

Nicko warms up backstage, Soundwave Festival, Brisbane.

2ND MARCH 2011. Bruce in the cockpit of ED FORCE ONE en route to Melbourne.

Janick at the Melbourne Aquarium.

The band and Killer Krew.

Nicko and Janick visit HMAS *Waller*, one of the largest Diesel-Electric submarines in the world.

Commander Peter Foster gives a guided tour of the ship, giving an intimate insight into life on board.

ABOVE: Nicko clambers down into the sub.

RIGHT: Janick and Nicko on the deck of HMAS *Waller*.

The visit is a morale boosting experience for the crew of the sub.

ABOVE: After exploring the control room, Nicko is shown the torpedo tubes and takes a large gasp of oxygen from an emergency air mask.

9TH MARCH 2011. Janick at the Bongeunsa Temple, Seoul, South Korea.

10TH MARCH 2011. Adrian and Dave make their way through the Olympic Stadium to the stage.

On a crisp clear morning in Seoul, ED FORCE ONE prepares for departure to Tokyo. The band are especially excited to be returning to Japan for two sell out shows. Little does anyone know the calm of Seoul is the quiet before the storm.

10:17
Japanese TV board ED FORCE ONE to film the flight to Tokyo.

10:54
Bruce is in a jovial mood in the cockpit.

12:25
The remaining band party are delayed and the departure time is put back by 35 minutes.

13:00
Flight 666 takes off from Seoul.

14:25
ED FORCE ONE begins its final descent into Tokyo.

14:46:23
Japan has the biggest earthquake in its recorded history, measuring a staggering 9.0. ED FORCE ONE is only 9 minutes away from landing.

14:51
Tokyo airport shuts down and issues a tsunami warning for the entire coast line. Diverted planes criss cross the sky as ED FORCE ONE regains altitude.

14:53
Bruce makes the announcement, 'there has been a massive earthquake below'.

14:59
Flight 666 is diverted to Nagoya.

15:25
ED FORCE ONE lands in Nagoya, 120 miles west of Tokyo.

Everyone stays on board whilst the band and production team discuss what to do next. At this stage the scale of the disaster is not fully known and the band want to do everything they can to play Tokyo. News slowly filters through of the devastation and it dawns on everyone how close ED FORCE ONE was to being on the ground at the time of the quake. The Japanese TV crew, who are still on board, have a translator who assists the production team in securing transport and accommodation in Nagoya.

Everyone's thoughts now turn to those affected by the quake and tsunami as Japanese television plays out the scenes of destruction.

There is little public transport, power supplies are severely affected and there is damage to numerous buildings. The Japanese promoter officially cancels the shows.

ED FORCE ONE sadly departs for Hawaii the following day. The concerned band and crew offer their condolences to the good people of Japan as the tragedy continues to unfold.

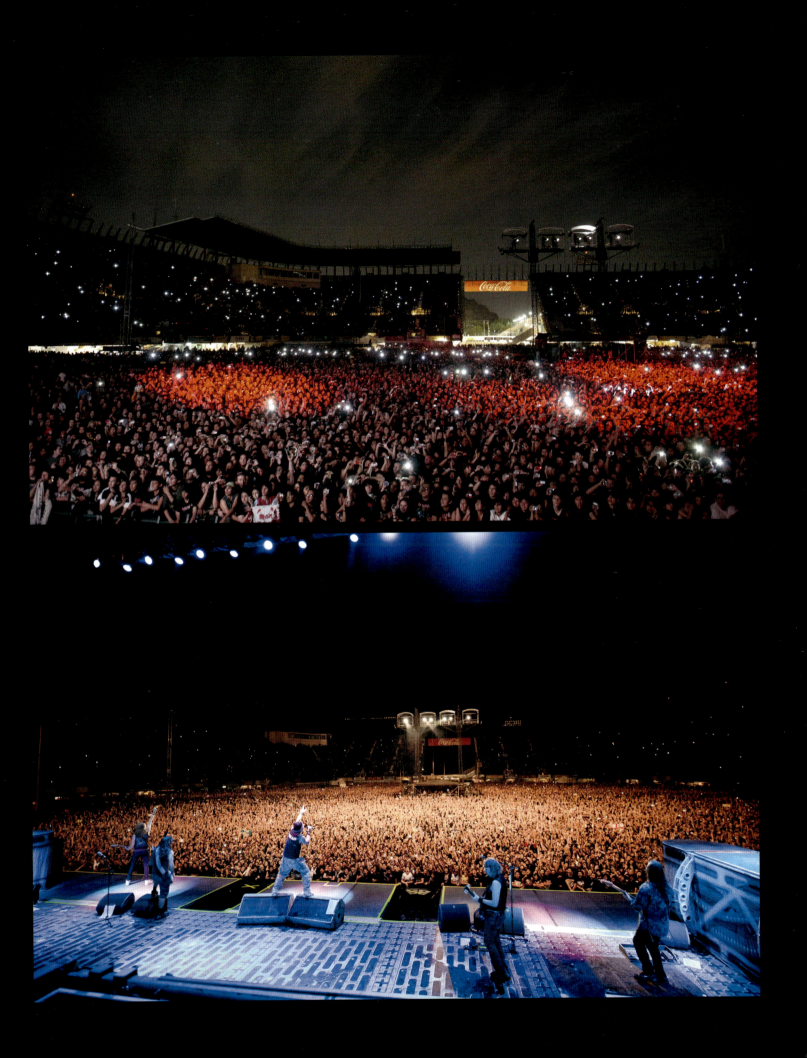

Tensions run high on the streets of Bogota but the mood inside the concert is one of celebration.

The day before the show, Bruce is invited by the Sao Paulo police to the local gun range. In a secret location underground an entire arsenal of weapons is made available for target practice.

NEXT PAGE: As the song 'Iron Maiden' plays out the set, two giant fingers appear either side of the stage, followed by a giant Eddie head snarling at the audience. The surprised fans are the first in the world to see the new 'Big Eddie'.

The Killer Krew travel overnight from Sao Paulo by road to build the show in time for the concert that evening – whilst ED FORCE ONE touches down at Rio De Janeiro airport on the day of the show. The band launch on to the stage at 9pm in front of a sold out HSBC Arena.

WE'RE STILL HERE

Seconds into the first song 'The Final Frontier', it is clear there is something very wrong at the front of the audience: the crowd barrier has collapsed, narrowly missing several of IRON MAIDEN's crew in the pit. The band stop playing and Bruce calms the crowd down and instructs everyone to take a step back. The crowd move back and security move in to attempt to fix the barrier. The metal work has splintered and buckled and is beyond repair but fortunately no one is injured. IRON MAIDEN refuse to put the crowd's safety at risk by continuing with the concert and vow to return the following night. With the local promotor to translate, Bruce walks back out on stage and explains the situation to the audience. IRON MAIDEN replace the venue's barrier and the band play to a relieved crowd the next night.

The ED FORCE ONE flight crew are told on approach to Belem that there are massive crowds forming at the airport and security are beginning to voice their concerns. As the excitement gathers in the terminal, military police hastily escort the band directly out of the airport and on to the busy roads of Belem. Flanked by several police outriders, the Maiden cavalcade is soon shadowed by fans in cars and on motorbikes. Approaching the Hilton Hotel, the streets narrow and the sheer size of the crowd celebrating the band's arrival stops the traffic.

The military police already struggling to contain the crowds advise against trying to enter the hotel through the front doors and promptly escort the vehicles to the rear of the hotel. Once in position the police create a human barrier, allowing the band entry through the kitchens. BELOW: Steve is escorted into the hotel by security.

Military police guard ED FORCE ONE, Curitiba, Brazil.

2011 ED FORCE ONE flight crew. Claudine Booth, Ana Belen Ilanes Bravo, Santiago Guerra Arranz, Bruce Dickinson, Kristian Winje, Tom Wilson, Fernando de Freitas, Gloria Vazquez Lopez.

ED FORCE ONE

IRON MAIDEN

6TH APRIL 2011. Curitiba, Brazil.

8TH APRIL 2011. Velez Sarsfield Stadium, Buenos Aires, Argentina.

ABOVE: ED FORCE ONE takes off from Buenos Aires.

TOP RIGHT: Dave Murray.

RIGHT: Ground crew at Santiago International Airport greet IRON MAIDEN.

TOP LEFT: Bruce plays the opening bars to 'The Trooper' on a Kazoo as ground transportation takes the band closer to the waiting crowd outside the airport.

ABOVE and LEFT: Bruce Dickinson Kart racing in Santiago.

14TH APRIL 2011. Coliseo de Puerto Rico, San Juan, Puerto Rico.

IRON MAIDEN management; Rod Smallwood and Andy Taylor arrive in Ft Lauderdale for the penultimate show of the tour.

First To The Barrier competition winners at Ft Lauderdale.

ABOVE: IRON MAIDEN walk on stage for the final show of the Around The World In 66 Days tour.

BELOW: Before introducing the song 'Blood Brothers', Bruce reminds every one that no one is excluded from the Maiden family.

After finishing their Final Frontier tour in London on 6th August 2011, IRON MAIDEN will have played to 2.3 million people, across 5 continents and 37 different countries, having visited a staggering 94 cities on this tour alone.

Bruce flies the final 4574 miles home.

ED FORCE ONE returns to Stansted airport after a gruelling but spectacular 66 day tour.

RIGHT: ED FORCE ONE refuels in Bermuda.

6:45AM: ED FORCE ONE makes its final approach towards Stansted Airport, England.

7:05AM: Stansted Airport, England.

When I stand before you showing
In the early morning sun
When I feel the engines roar
And I think of what we've
done.

Coming home far away
As the vapour trails alight
Where I've been tonight
You know I will not stay

(The singer
bloke)

6TH AUGUST 2011. O2 Arena, London, England. The Last Show Of The Final Frontier Tour.
Over the whole touring period, including both tours, the band have travelled over 200, 000 miles,
performing in 127 different cities, visiting 52 countries and playing to over 4 million fans.

IRON MAIDEN WOULD LIKE TO THANK YOU, THE FANS, FOR BEING THERE AND MAKING ALL OF THIS POSSIBLE.

First published in Great Britain in 2011
by Orion
This paperback edition published in 2014
by Orion Books Ltd,
Orion House, 5 Upper St Martin's Lane,
London WC2H 9EA

10 9 8 7 6 5 4 3 2 1

A CIP catalogue record for this book is available
from the British Library.

ISBN: 978-1-4091-3759-7

Printed in China

The Orion Publishing Group's policy is to use papers
that are natural, renewable and recyclable and made
from wood grown in sustainable forests. The logging
and manufacturing processes are expected to
conform to the environmental regulations of the
country of origin.

Every effort has been made to fulfil requirements with
regard to reproducing copyright material. The author
and publisher will be glad to rectify any omissions at
the earliest opportunity.

www.orionbooks.co.uk

John McMurtrie would like to thank:

My adorable wife Jo and my superheroes Miles & Archie.

Bruce Dickinson, Steve Harris, Janick Gers,
Dave Murray, Adrian Smith and Nicko McBrain.
Rod Smallwood and Andy Taylor.
Val Janes for all her help and support with this project.
Mary Henry, Pete De Vroome, Aky Najeeb,
Katherine Pedder, Sarah Philp and everyone at
Phantom Management.
Ian Day, Steve Gadd, Dickie Bell, Patrick Ledwith
and all the Iron Maiden Killer Krew.

John Mahon, Fernando de Freitas and all the Astraeus
crew, past and present.
Jeremy Smith at ROCK-IT Cargo.
Jim Eames at ATL .
Everyone at Nikon Worldwide especially Jeremy Gilbert
at Nikon UK for his continued support.
Michael Dover, Rowland White, Jillian Young, Helen Ewing,
Mark Rusher, Mark Stay, Elizabeth Allen and Debbie
Woska at Orion Publishing.
Alex & Emma Smith at Smith & Gilmour.
Roo Ball at Allied Photolabs/Display.
James Isaacs, Alexander Milas, Chris Ingham and
everyone at *Metal Hammer* Magazine.
Will Luff and Paul Fletcher at EMI.
Chris Ayres.
Matt Munday.
Daniel Lezano.
David Beck at the Flash Centre.
Johnny 'Skywire' Burke.
Dave Pattenden.
Martin Hawkes, Frank 'the shot' Shortt, Sam Dunn,
Scot McFadyen, Kevin Mackenzie and all at Banger Films.
Lauren Harris, Kerry Harris, Richie Faulkner,
Randy Gregg, Tommy McWilliams, Ollie Smith.
Rise to Remain.
Jeannie Aquino and Mike Massimino at NASA Houston.
Monkey and Patten.
The Norse – Hughes, Anstis, Lovett & Bushell.
The McMurtrie family.
Lexar, Adobe Lightroom, Elinchrom and Tamrac.

YOU ALL ROCK!

www.johnmcmurtrie.co.uk
www.ironmaiden.com